7 ESSENTIAL SKILLS OF LEADERSHIP

How To Lead Your Organization To Operational Excellence

Jeff Adams

First edition of this book published in 2016
Management & Leadership
ISBN 978-0-9979682-1-7

www.continuousleadership.com

To my wife, Beth.
She has been a constant inspiration to me, and
has always supported me in my endeavors. A man couldn't
ask for a better life partner.

CONTENTS

ACKNOWLEDGMENTS

While I would love to say that the material within these pages came solely from my brilliant mind, I cannot. One of my sayings is, "No one ever accused me of being a genius," and that still holds true. The 7 Essential Skills, their application, and the stories and examples that go along with sharing them, are a combination of my personal experiences in business as well as the vast amount of personal study and training I've had over the years concerning leadership, process improvement, continuous improvement, and operational excellence. Not to be forgotten is the interaction I've had with some fantastic co-workers over the years that have influenced the development of these 7 Essential Skills. I cannot claim the contents are totally original, but they are packaged in a manner that comes from my perspective and presented in a way that I believe makes the information easily usable.

While I have made notes in the *Notes* and *Sources for Self-Development* sections on sources, and made every effort to give credit to those who have gone before me and provided much of the foundation for my development of the 7 Essential Skills, there are three individuals who deserve special recognition:

Gary Kirsch – My boss at the time the 7 Essential Skills began to be formed and went from a conversation to a fully developed concept. Gary encouraged me in my pursuit of building on the concepts and provided regular feedback on my development of the presentation of these skills. Without his encouragement and regular feedback, I'm not sure this book would have come to fruition. Gary saw the potential in the 7 Essential Skills as much as I did, if not more.

Bill McCormick – My co-worker during this same time, and mentor in my pursuit of knowledge in continuous improvement as well as several of my certifications in Lean, Six Sigma, and Quick Response Manufacturing (QRM). The hours of conversation on methodologies, application of those methodologies, sharing of stories, his patience and sage advice at work and on developing the 7 Essential Skills were invaluable.

Ashley Tish - My employee and mentee, again during the time in which I started working on the 7 Essential Skills. Ashley was a millennial among "geezers," but held her own in providing great insight and constructive criticism on my development of the 7 Essential Skills. Gary, Bill, and I were the veterans; weathered, experienced, and optimistic while realistic. Ashley was a shining, shooting star, still full of excitement with unlimited possibilities, and her insights from a new generation were a shot in the arm for this crusty, "seasoned" individual.

INTRODUCTION

Like many business books, this one was born out of an identified business need. Probably unlike many of those other books, the idea didn't start out with the concept, "We need a book about this," but rather was generated through a chain of events and identifying evolving needs. The concept came about while working as part of a continuous improvement group within a large organization. We were tasked with handling improvement projects out at various facilities within the company. These projects had varying levels of success, depending on the local support we got. However, the improvements did not seem to last. I suggested to my boss, Gary Kirsch, that what we needed to do was educate people at the facilities in the basics of continuous improvement concepts (specifically Lean methodology) so they could help us, understand what we were talking about, and sustain the improvements when we left. Gary, Bill McCormick, and I went to work on developing a Lean course that would provide people with the knowledge and tools to implement continuous improvement efforts at their facilities. Our foundation for developing this course was the Body of Knowledge for Lean Bronze Certification provided by SME (Society of Manufacturing Engineers).

The course proved fairly successful. Over a two-year period, over 160 people across the company went through our Lean course. Not only were people more helpful when we went into facilities, but our students were conducting projects themselves, and there was success in their efforts. However, we noticed some locations were having issues with sustaining the changes. When investigating why this was, we found some of our students complained that they weren't getting support from their upper management. It was easy to see the sustaining facilities had management support, while the non-sustaining facilities did not. This difference in sustainment was confirmation of what I had read, as well as what I had experienced in the past. There was a need to educate managers on how to support a continuous improvement environment.

I started looking at my past experiences, successes and failures, and analyzing what we were observing. This was the drive for developing the 7 Essential Skills. I resolved to come up with as simple an approach as I could to communicate the basics that management would have to do to act like leaders with their people. I sought feedback from people I knew would be constructively honest with my idea: Gary, Bill, and Ashley. With their input, the basic concepts were outlined. From there, this book was developed.

A note on implementing the 7 Essential Skills: The key to successful implementation of these skills is to blitz the entire management of a single facility. While individually reading this book, and applying it yourself will improve your personal performance as a leader, you will find these skills much more effective if everyone on the leadership team is on the same page. If you are attempting this on your own, the struggle can be much harder to change how your organization functions. This is not just about process improvement, continuous improvement, or even Operational Excellence. This is about culture change, which incorporates all of these. Managers need to be leaders (yes, there is a difference), and drive the kind of behaviors that promote Operational Excellence, which changes how people think and act, and that in turn changes the culture.

I'm the kind of person that when I buy into something, it's hard to let go. This idea of needing to develop leadership kept gnawing at me. My wife and I discussed the pattern I had seen repeatedly over time; a failure of management/leadership to develop their people for management positions.

Upper management tends to perpetuate a system of management that is flawed at best, failing at worst. Organizations need to develop leaders, not managers. I kept saying how if I could just get people to listen to the ideas of the 7 Essential Skills, I was sure I could help organizations turn things around. Finally, the idea of writing a book composed of these 7 Essential Skills "came" to me when my wife was listening to me talk one evening about the need for these skills while we were preparing supper, and she blurted out, "You need to write a book about all of this." God bless her. I was talking so much about what needed to be done with leadership, I didn't see an obvious approach to sharing the information. I needed to document these skills in a format that would make it not only available to anyone who wanted to be a leader and tackle Operational Excellence, but do so in a fashion that didn't read like some school text book; thorough enough to provide what a person would need to implement these skills, but also a short enough read to hold their attention.

This book is intended for those in leadership positions, or those who desire to be in leadership positions, who want to establish a continuous improvement culture within their organization with the desire to achieve Operational Excellence. For this reason, I've made the assumption that the reader will already have some working familiarity with the various continuous improvement methodologies (Lean, Six Sigma, TOC, BPM, QRM, etc.) and I won't be going into any real detail on those methodologies. The goal here is to help leadership behave like leaders in a continuous improvement environment. I've repeatedly run into management at various levels of organizations who want change without changing themselves. Simply put, that does not work. It leads to limited success at best, and thus the organization is more frustrated after the failed attempt at continuous improvement than it was before.

I believe it is important to state up front that I do not believe that the material within this book provides unique revelations on how to be successful as a leader. The information here is gleaned from me having studied leadership in my R.O.T.C. classes in college, and during my time as an officer in the U.S. Air Force, along with countless seminars in private industry. In addition, there is my personal reading of numerous books, and discussions with others pursuing self-development in the area of leadership. I've had many conversations on leadership with people who have achieved senior positions in organizations, and I find much repetition in many sources. What you will find in these pages is the summation of my years, even decades, of studying, learning (in class and by practical experience), and practical application. That knowledge and experience is all boiled down to the fundamental essence of what one needs to do if one wants to be a good leader when pursuing Operational Excellence.

It is important that people understand that there are two types of people who run things (aren't there always two types?): Managers and Leaders. There is an old saying, "you manage things, but you lead people." It is possible to be a good manager, but a lousy leader, something I've seen a lot of over the years. I believe it's also possible to be a good leader and lousy manager. If I had to pick between the two, I'd want a leader. If people report to you, you need to be a good leader. My hope in writing this book is that those who choose to read it will find something that will help them become better leaders. If anyone reports to you, wake up, you are a leader by default. Not everyone is going to be a great leader, but you can be a better leader if you work to apply the 7 Essential Skills presented here.

I once worked for an executive who exemplified several key leadership traits. When he took over the organization I was in, the workforce was largely demotivated. Within a month of taking over, he had people excited about the possibilities of the organization turning around, and the direction we were headed. He was doing everything I had been advocating to his predecessor in my role as Change Manager, but had been flatly rejected. I was quite excited about what was happening. During one conversation with this executive, I discovered that while we agreed on many things to make the organization function better, we had one area where we radically disagreed: Leadership. He was adamant that you were either born with the ability or you weren't. I believe that one might have some natural talent, but someone who had no leadership traits can

4

develop them if they are willing to work at it. My boss rejected this as an impossibility. I didn't argue, but I was unconvinced of his view. If you either are a leader or you are not, and you can do nothing to change that, then all the leadership books, all the leadership courses, all the leadership tools, and all the videos on leadership are a total waste of time and a complete rip off of those who spent good money on them. I am unwavering in my belief that anyone, *anyone*, can be a better leader if they are willing to work at it. I'm not saying you'll necessarily be a great leader, but you can be better than you are today. These 7 Essential Skills will help you with becoming that better leader.

In my years of working with continuous improvement concepts, it never fails that management wants help in making things better in their department, facility, division, etc. That said, it is rare that one finds a manager who is asking for help will also be willing to do something himself/herself. Usually, they want a process improvement person, or team, to come in, overhaul their processes, "fix" everything, and then leave. Meanwhile, that senior person does nothing to help implement or maintain the changes. In this scenario, give it anywhere from two weeks to six months, and everything will migrate back to the way it was before, and it will be as if your process improvement person/people had never been there. Then comes the standard comment, "See, I told you that improvement stuff doesn't work."

What didn't work was the leadership. I've had experiences where organizations were dysfunctional and the leadership asked our team to come in and help, and once we started doing things, and people got excited, we turned to the leadership (this could be the leadership team as a whole, or an individual) and said, "Now, here is what you need to do," only to be stopped and told by the leadership that they have no intention of changing how *they* do anything. We once had a high level executive at this point simply ask us to leave, saying they weren't going to change, and they'd stick to the path they were on (one that was losing market share and profit margin by the way). This individual was a high-powered *manager*, but in no way were they a leader.

In situations where there is management, but no leaders, you usually have a workforce that is uninspired, unmotivated, and performs marginally at best. In this state, your good employees will search out new opportunities outside the company, leaving you with substandard performers who either couldn't find work elsewhere, or worse, are so lazy they don't even bother to look. These remaining individuals will usually end up doing the minimum to collect a paycheck while avoiding getting fired until the business performs so poorly it shuts its doors and they finally *have* to go looking for work. This is not only no way to run a business, this is no way to live. Leaders should be inspiring their people so they are excited about coming to work, and what they do. The greatest asset, and most untapped resource, any business has is its people. Lead them.

Over time, through experience as well as studies, I have found that if you want to achieve excellence in your business, you have to lead people. It doesn't just happen by keeping the paperwork moving. How you lead people makes a difference. In the following pages I will lay out 7 Essential Leadership Skills that you can use to inspire, motivate, develop, and truly lead your people to Operational Excellence. Study and practice these skills. The more you work at them, the better you'll become at applying them. This book is the beginning of a journey towards not just being a leader, but being a great leader. You will have to continue your development beyond what you read in these pages here, and I've made some recommendations for more reading at the end. Again, if you have people reporting to you, by default you are a leader. Become a better leader by using these 7 Essential Skills to better your people. Grow together as a team, as a company, and you'll have the success you are looking for.

DEFINING OPERATIONAL EXCELLENCE AND LEADERSHIP'S ROLE

"If we chase perfection we can catch excellence."
— Vince Lombardi

To start with, what is Operational Excellence? In his book, Design for Operational Excellence, Kevin Duggan gives one of the best definitions I've seen. Duggan defines Operational Excellence as when "Each and every employee can see the flow of value to the customer and fix that flow before it breaks down."[1] This epitomizes a high functioning team where everyone knows his/her job, is empowered to do what needs to be done to make things happen without fear of reprisal for taking the initiative, and management isn't spending its time firefighting.

Operational Excellence isn't perfection, but it does minimize the flaws, imperfections, and bumps in the road that any organization will experience. Establishing excellence in how we do things can mean the difference between a ripple in the water of our operations that might interrupt the flow of things, and a tidal wave that wipes you out. That may sound dramatic, but in an economic downturn, or the rise of a serious competitor, Operational Excellence can mean the difference between survival and the collapse of your business. Operational Excellence doesn't happen by chance. People have to be led to the goal of Operational Excellence.

Ironically, when people study business in school, they are studying business *management*. This deals with how to handle financials, purchasing, inventory, calculating production capacity, etc. Rarely, if ever, do they study business *leadership*. My observation is that people learn how to run a business based purely on the numbers according to traditional accounting practices, and are influenced in larger businesses by the pressures of a board and stockholders to produce quarterly and annual numbers that make these people happy. In the short term, this provides dividends to the stockholders, but in the long term the actions these pressures force are not necessarily positive for the future health of the organization. My analogy is to compare this to politics in the U.S. Politicians typically make decisions and take actions that will help them win the next election cycle, not necessarily what is good for the long term health of the country. An example of this is the federal government's inability to take actions that properly deal with our growing national debt.

If one is going to be a leader and bring about Operational Excellence, you will have to do what is often counter intuitive to the traditional way of handling business. Think long term and let that guide your actions. Work with upper management (and they in turn with the board and shareholders) to take the long view, rather than just trying to make people happy this quarter. Step up and lead.

Leadership can be situational. Depending on the personnel you have, their skill sets, and the current culture, all of this can impact how you should handle exerting your leadership, and whether you will be successful or not. There are leaders, who in one situation are very successful, and in others they fail miserably. This is often because they did not modify their leadership style to fit the situation. To be consistently successful at leadership, you must be flexible in how you exercise that leadership. This means you need to know your people, know the environment, have a vision of where you want to go, and develop a plan that will get you there. Tools and skills are transferable, but this is not a cookie-cutter scenario. Each person, each team, each organization will have its own unique challenges. It may look the same, and even sound the same, but there can be subtle differences that require very different applications of leadership styles and skills. (I will expand on this in the *Collaboration* section.)

Leadership's role is to cultivate a culture of Operational Excellence.

In creating and nurturing this kind of culture, you will end up creating teams of empowered, engaged, and involved employees that embrace the opportunities to identify and solve the issues that crop up in the workplace. The rewards for bringing this kind of culture to life will be employees who love coming to work, feel a sense of ownership, and therefore loyalty for the company, and to their leader. (That's you!)

There are certain characteristics of an Operational Excellence culture. Among those characteristics is leadership that is always learning, whether by self-development or via professional development. These leaders will also be engaged in coaching and mentoring the members of their organization, and are adaptable to change, not stuck in the current way of doing things, thinking this will carry them through for the rest of their career. The management/leadership team is fully engaged and committed to the concept of Operational Excellence. Leadership will make the voice of the customer a key aspect of what drives their actions in their business. They will be constantly fostering an environment that delivers results that are responsive to the voice of the customer. They show respect for others, and challenge people to strive to constantly improve themselves. And leaders will apply lessons learned from every "failure." On this last item, you cannot play the blame game. You must look at issues instead of people, and search for the true root cause for why excellence wasn't achieved, then address that issue so it doesn't reoccur. Working with your people in pursuing the elimination of these issues helps to build this culture of Operational Excellence.

There are a lot of tools that can be used to help you achieve Operational Excellence. Continuous Improvement methodologies, such as Lean, Six Sigma, Theory of Constraints, Quick Response Manufacturing (QRM), Business Process Management (BPM), and others are readily available to apply in helping you achieve Operational Excellence. I'm not going to advocate one methodology over another, although I do have my biases like anyone else familiar with these methodologies. The reason I'm leaving the methodology of choice up to you is because what is truly important is that you find what tools work best for your business, and what methodology you are most comfortable using. Like many things, sometimes a mix of tools from various methodologies can be helpful, but you the reader will know your business best, and are therefore in a better position to know what will work for your organization.

Whichever methodology, or mix of methodologies, you decide on, the 7 Essential Skills will prove invaluable in making your continuous improvement efforts successful, and will be an integral part of your Operational Excellence culture. Remember, you will be creating a business culture where the environment is one where people are encouraged to continue to learn and grow. All your people will become problem solvers, and will be encouraged to experiment with improving their processes within defined boundaries.

Mistakes aren't used for punishment, but rather as opportunities for learning. You need to recognize your people for group and individual efforts, and everyone should hold themselves and each other accountable for everyday problem solving.

Your willingness and ability to embrace and apply the 7 Essential Skills will determine your organization's success in achieving Operational Excellence. These skills are surprisingly simple, but not necessarily easy to make a part of your leadership style. Remember the saying, "Opportunities often come disguised as work." It will be work to develop these skills, as with any new skill. However, even if you are not very smooth in their application at first, they will have a positive impact on your business. And as with any skill, the more your practice and apply these skills, the better you will get at employing them. In time, they will become a part of you and how you lead.

SKILL 1: ESTABLISHING THE GOAL

"You've got to be very careful if you don't know where you are going, because you might not get there."
— *Yogi Berra*

It's surprising how most companies have rather vague mission statements that are supposed to guide them. Often, I think these mission statements, or company visions, are more fluff for board members and stockholders rather than actual goals that drive company performance. Even if an organization has taken the time to truly develop some strategic goals, they rarely are shared beyond the people who created them. I'm not talking about having them posted on a wall somewhere, or sending out a mass e-mail. I mean really shared and explained to people so they understand not only what the goals are, but what their role is in achieving those goals.

So why do we even bother establishing goals? Goals provide a direction in which an organization can work as a cohesive unit to move toward. Leaders need to promote and encourage their team members to get involved in pursuing these goals. Team members should be able to connect with the goals so that they feel some level of commitment to achieving them, and are motivated to engage in activities that support these goals.

You need an effective strategy to establishing goals. Here are some key elements to an effective strategy:

1. Know your customer's requirements; know your organization's purpose and mission. Question: Does your organization's purpose and mission relate, in any way, to your customer's requirements? If

not, perhaps you should take the time to talk to your customer and revise your purpose and mission to meet their needs.

2. Do you have some core values and principles that you actually live and function by? If not, you'll need to develop some. If asked, can people at every level of your organization tell you what those core values and principles are? Do they relate to them? Can they say that they, and the people they work with, live out those values and principles?

3. Have challenging expectations of your people and your organization. Not unrealistic, but high enough to keep your people stretching themselves. In setting stretch goals, make sure they are in alignment with your purpose, mission, values, and principles.

4. Deploy the strategy with measureable goals, and ensure there is consensus across all functions on those goals and how they are measured.

You need to remember that in deploying your strategy you will want to drive your vision/goals down to the tactics that align actions throughout the organization to achieve results. Some questions to ask are:

1. What is your purpose or mission?
2. What is your future state vision?
3. What are your strategic goals?
4. What are this year's goals?
5. How can we "water fall" these goals down?

By "water fall," I mean how can the next level down in the organization operate in such a fashion that their actions support the goals of the level above them? Typically, this means that when the higher level in the organization has specific goals, they establish action items to support those goals, the next level down will take those action items and make them their goals, and then develop action items to support their established goals. Pictorially it would look something like this:

"Water Fall" Strategies and Goals

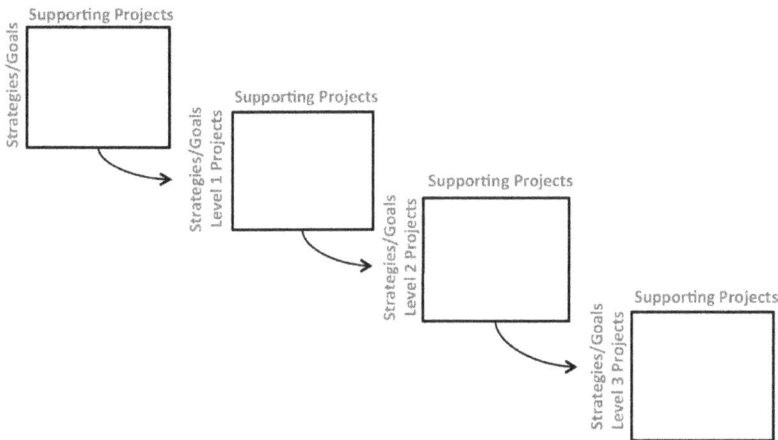

This example shouldn't be misconstrued to mean that goals are set 'on high' and everyone must simply submit to whatever comes their way and work with it. There should be interaction across management levels, where ideas are shared. A term used for this is "catchball," with the analogy to tossing a ball back and forth. In this case, the "ball" is ideas for goals. Another way of looking at it is upper management makes proposed goals, and lower management makes a "counter offer" on what they think is reasonable, or impactful for achieving overall operational goals. This can go several rounds until consensus is reached on goals all can support. It is important that everyone has buy-in to the established goals so there is ownership and commitment to achieving those goals.

At each level of an organization, as they establish their goals and action items, they should make sure that they fully understand how their actions impact their goals, who is involved (and how), and how they are measuring their performance. An excellent tool for engaging your team and helping them appreciate the goals, and their impact on them, is the X-matrix, which looks like this:

STRATEGY DEPLOYMENT FOR YEAR _____ OWNERSHIP

Determine reorder point levels & EOQS
Develop supplier strategy
Develop client strategy plan
Capacity/resource planning
Implement 5S entire facility
Cycle count 100%
Kardex shuttle project
Re-establish past metrics (on hold end of Q1)

Improvement Projects/Goals (How?)

Strategic Vision/Objectives (What?)

Targets/Metrics

Impact (Why?)

$81 million in sales (20% OP)

Reduce spares lead time and improve on-time delivery
Which sales success
Reduce capital expenses lead time and improve on-time delivery
Stock control/Accuracy

Stock value/ month (18 M)
Stock accuracy less < 2.5% deviation
Capital: OTD 90% (< 10 days still on time)
LW PcE: Lead time 8 weeks
Winch lead time reduction by 25% (current 14 weeks)
Confirmed orders per month: 4 winches
Spares: lead time reduction by 50% (current 40 days)
Spares: OTD 75% < 3 days late (current 60% <3 days late)

TBD
Brian
Jake
Robert
Cindy
Francis
Lisa
William
Larry
Lean Team
Joe

START!

Correlation Legend	
Relationship	
O	Very strong
⊖	Important
Δ	Weak

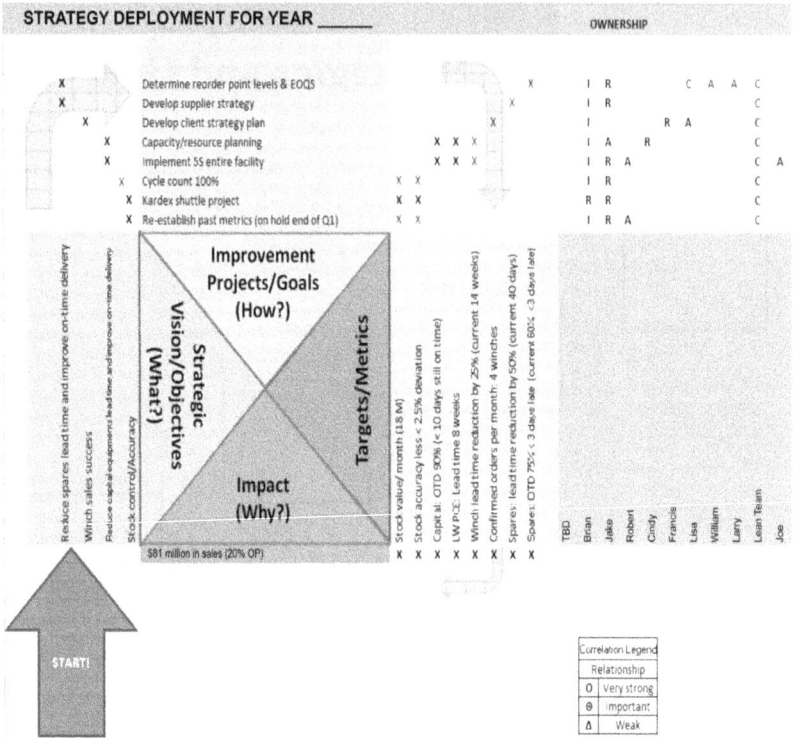

In the X-matrix, you begin by writing down your strategic goals (where the "start" arrow is). Going around the matrix clockwise, you then identify the action items/projects to support the strategic goals (across the top of the matrix). Next you come down the right side of the matrix and identify how you will measure the performance of your action items/projects, and finally tie the measurements to the impact, or financial results you desire (across the bottom of the matrix). The relationship between a particular goal and a project is marked with an 'X' in the white quadrant between goals and projects, and relationships between projects and measurements, and same for measurements and financial impacts. The far right section of the matrix is usually used to identify project owners and put an 'X' correlating between the project owner and the project. In this example, the concept of the "RACI" diagram is incorporated. This way, you can not only identify on each project who is Responsible, but also who is Accountable, Consulted, and Informed.

The X-matrix can be developed for one level, and the projects selected can be shared with the next level down to help them in building their own X-matrix. Such as this:

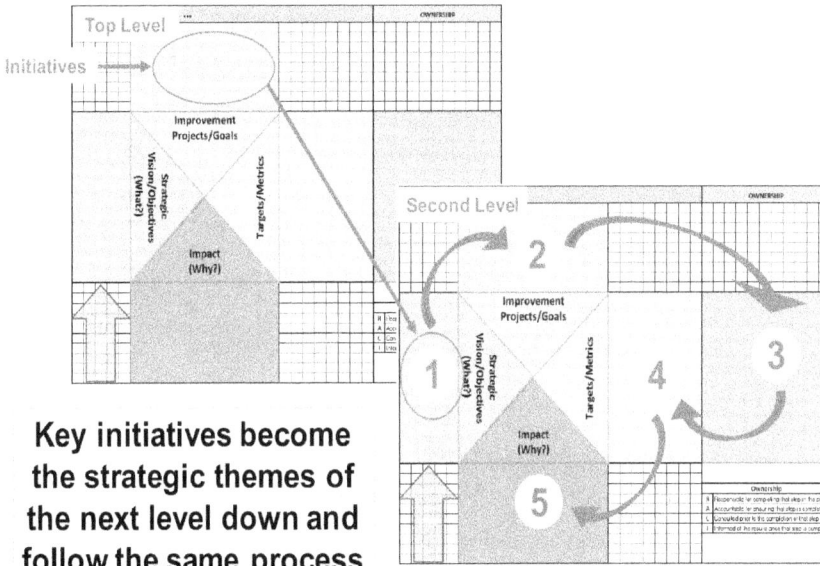

Key initiatives become the strategic themes of the next level down and follow the same process

When you use this approach, you help focus your people on the vital few issues and actions that will lead your team to success as you have defined it. Working as a team to develop this strategy, and deploying it together, communicates a shared vision and creates alignment through participation. This all helps to encourage cross functional cooperation, and ensures mutual success. Planning is systemic, and thus your people will find themselves working as a team.

SKILL 2: HANDLING CHANGE

"And one should bear in mind that there is nothing more difficult to execute, nor more dubious of success, nor more dangerous to administer, than to introduce a new order of things; for he who introduces it has all those who profit from the old order as his enemies, and he has only lukewarm allies in all those who might profit from the new."
— *Machiavelli on Change*

The late Edwards Deming once said, "It is not necessary to change. Survival is not mandatory." Change is inevitable. Whether you are willing to embrace that change and be proactive in addressing it, or resist change and are forced into a reactive mode about addressing the change is your choice. You can also choose to ignore the change and continue doing what you have always done and suffer the consequences. What you decide here will determine if you and your organization thrive, survive, or die.

What forces can drive change? The most obvious force is competition. Various businesses will offer the same product, or similar products, all saying theirs is the best. You need to strive to change how your organization functions so you can stay competitive and profitable. When the economy turns up or down, your business is impacted and this requires you to change how you do things. The political environment can sometimes make or break you if you aren't looking ahead and anticipating the needed changes to survive the actions of politicians. The global marketplace can impact you significantly. The more free trade agreements the United States gets into, the tougher the competition is when wages overseas are usually much lower than here at home. What demographics are you aiming your product at? This can make a big difference in how you function, especially assuming you want to catch part of each new generation, you need to understand their needs and desires. Then there are social and ethical issues that can drive change. Being a "good corporate citizen" is a nice way of saying people want the company they buy from to be environmentally responsible and to avoid child labor overseas.

A leader will acknowledge that change is coming, or is here, and will be proactive in addressing that change. One thing a leader must be able to do is assess the readiness of his people to embrace change. If you are in an environment that doesn't engage the workforce, and people don't feel like part of a team, but are merely employees, I would suspect that no one is ready to jump on board the "change train." In fact, you'll have tremendous resistance, and you will have to work on the fundamentals of developing the team mentality to prepare people for change. You are already behind the power curve, and potentially in big trouble if the change is coming fast. If on the other hand you do have a team atmosphere in your organization, in part or whole, you can pull together identified resources and people to help shape your organization to prepare for change and drive to the future state that meets the challenge.

Something else a leader must be able to do is gage the agility of their team to quickly and effectively focus their energy and implement change. Do you have an established standard method for implementing new processes, or modifying current processes? Does everyone on your team know how this works, the tools to use, how to document activities and who is accountable for what by when? An agile team knows these things. An agile team is ready for change.

Look over your organization and see what kind of environment you have. Is it ready for change? Here are some indicators of an organization that is not ready for change:

1. Rewards "firefighting." I call this the "Hero stage." If your people, and especially your management team, spend their days putting out fires and "saving the day" getting orders out the door, then you are in a constant reaction mode. This is just the kind of place that needs change, but no one thinks they have time to put any focus

on changing things. They are right in the sense that their poor time management and lack of leadership skills give them no time to devote to improving things. They are also wrong because they desperately need to change things, and with a little determination and self-discipline they can find time to make it happen.

2. General mentality is "don't rock the boat." This kind of environment usually comes from repeated events where someone "mistakenly" thinks they can offer a suggestion, only to find out that they get shouted down, or "put in their place."

> I once saw a young machinist try to point out an opportunity to improve how they were doing setups to the chief Industrial Engineer in a plant. The response startled me as much as it did the young machinist. The chief IE said, "Your job is not to think! You cut metal! I'm the engineer, and I'll make things better for you! Get back to work and shut up!" Hard to believe that kind of "leadership" still exists in the 21st century, but it's more prevalent than some realize. The machinist went back to work, and I went over to talk to him to see if he was okay. His only comment was, "I'll never bring anything up ever again." A valuable resource was lost to this organization that day in the form of an employee whose spirit was crushed.

3. Why change? This mentality usually comes from people who think, "We are making money and no one's complaining (much), so why do anything different?" Whether rooted in short term thinking, or an attitude that they think customers have nowhere else to go (but they usually do), it overlooks a key aspect of Operational Excellence and every continuous improvement methodology: Listen to the Voice of the Customer (this can be an internal customer of your organization, or an external customer). If you aren't listening to the needs of the customer, even if you are building a quality product and getting it out on time, if it isn't what the customer wants, you've lost.

4. "I got where I am in this business doing it this way for 20 years,

why change now?" As our economy and culture keep picking up the speed at which technology changes, new products are released, and customers desires and needs change, you can't afford to assume what worked yesterday is going to work tomorrow. This stuck in a rut mentality is a sure fire way to put your organization behind the power curve and lose market share and find yourself quickly out of business. What worked two years ago is most likely antiquated today.

5. People are in a comfort zone. Even if they are unhappy and unfulfilled in their jobs, people often resist change because it takes them out of a known situation into an unknown situation, and that can be uncomfortable. This is also a key reason why even when you make changes, without proper leadership, people drift back to those old bad habits, into their comfort zone, undoing the changes that were made.

What about individual resistance to change? Beyond the environment you and the rest of your leadership team have developed (yes, you need to own the environment, good or bad), why would the people themselves as individuals resist change? Here are a few reasons I've found over the years:

1. Uncertainty and insecurity. As mentioned before, change can bring on the unknown, and this scares most people. Also, with change comes the fear of jobs being eliminated, and no one wants to "improve" things to the point they work themselves out of a job.

2. Selective perception and retention. If you've tried some kind of process improvement effort before and things didn't go well, odds are most people will look at this effort as another "flavor of the month," even if things do start to change. Depending on how you launch the effort, you could drive off employees you would like to keep. How people see things, from their perspective is important and you as the leader need to understand and address their concerns.

3. Habit. I once had a friend who was very successful, financially and professionally, who made the comment, "Habits are easy to break.

It's just easier not to break them." How true. People resist change because they have established habit patterns that are familiar and they know them. Change means learning new things, and it's easier (in their mind) to stick with what you already know, rather than learn new things.

4. Threats to status, security, pay, job role, social environment. Change can appear to threaten the status quo, and those with power and are in the know could lose their perceived position. Everything could change. I encourage people to embrace change by pointing out that with change is a new opportunity to be the new person with knowledge, and to be on the cutting edge of the new paradigm, leading and making a name for himself or herself.

5. The change process itself. Making the effort to do things differently can create individual resistance. It's like exercising. Getting started can be tough, but once you've developed the new habit of exercising, you hate to miss a workout.

In evaluating the readiness of your organization for change, you will need to look at the various groups within your organization, and even down to the individual level, and analyze where they are concerning change readiness, and identify who in each group is going to be a key stakeholder in driving change. In doing this, take a methodical approach and document the following information:

1. ID names of the key groups
2. Identify a trusted member of each group as a point of contact
3. Rate the group's degree of buy-in to change
4. Understand the issues and concerns of each group
5. Rate the importance to success of each group
6. Engage the group concerning the change (provide some orientation, training as required, get them involved, provide coaching as needed).

So you think your organization is ready for change. How do you maintain employee engagement and commitment when facing continuous change? How do you align your organization around strategic changes to insure efficient implementation? How do you build an organization that is capable of adapting to continuous change? How do you position your people, structure and strategy to come out of the current climate in a highly competitive state? Let's talk about it.

Organizational goals and strategies need to be properly aligned and shared with everyone so they know what direction you are headed in. They also need to know their role in achieving these goals and strategies. You need to have an organizational structure that supports those goals and strategies, along with proper policies and procedures fully documented and available for all to see and use. In addition, the physical setting of the workplace must be supportive to how you are changing things to support your goals and strategies (meaning environment, layout, availability of tools and materials, etc.). There needs to be some kind of rewards system in place to reinforce positive behavior/actions that support the new paradigm of how you want your organization to function. The reward system is one that is relevant to your organization. Having pictures of employee of the month on the wall, or handing out gift cards have limited value; I would suggest talking to your people and coming up with something more creative and relatable for your workforce.

I came across one organization that had a suggestion program. It was unlike any other I'd seen. If an employee had an idea for an improvement on a process or a product, the idea was submitted on a form, and a committee would review the idea for its viability. If it was decided the idea was worth going forward on, it was implemented, then the impact of the improvement on the business was tracked for 12 months. At the end of the 12 months, the financial impact/return on investment was calculated, and the employee was rewarded with a one-time check for 10% of the financial impact their idea had. Once a couple of employees started getting checks for their ideas, suggestions started flowing in, actually creating a backlog of suggestions for improvements the review committee had to review. For this organization, their reward program proved very powerful. Checks were cut for anywhere from $50 to $500, and some even as much as $10,000 to $27,000. The leadership held quarterly "celebrations" and publicly presented the checks to the employees. And the team reviewing suggestions had a backlog of over 150 ideas they were working their way through! This was a high performing organization where people enjoyed their work and workplace, and felt a sense of ownership. Change was constant due to all the suggestions for improvement, and profitability was high.

You also need to consider social factors, part of the culture of your organization. How do people tend to communicate or interact with one another? Is your organization very informal, or formal? These kinds of things will influence your management style, by which I mean do your communications with people sound more directive or consultative? If moving towards a team-based environment (which you will need to, to achieve Operational Excellence), you may have to modify your management style. If you don't already know, get to know the knowledge, skills, abilities, motivation, and behaviors of your people. This may have to change as well, as you change the culture of your organization. This part may sound obvious, but I am continuously struck by how upper management (even at a plant level) don't connect with their people and know nothing of their world view or what they go through at work every day. They are disconnected, but trying to manage (rather than lead) an organization they don't truly interact with.

In his book, "Leading Change," John Kotter provides an 8-step change model.[2] These eight steps, which he explains in detail, are a path to changing your organization, and give some guidance for how to lead that change. I'm not going to reprint everything here, but the eight steps for Kotter's model are as follows:

1. Create a Sense of Urgency
2. Form a Powerful Coalition
3. Create a Vision
4. Communicate the Vision
5. Remove the Obstacles

6.   Create Short-Term Wins

7.   Build on the Change

8.   Embed the Change into the Culture

I would offer a tool to go along with Kotter's 8-step process. I call it the "AIR Feedback Process." It's a simple communication tool that you can use when communicating with people and providing feedback. It works for both positive and constructive feedback, and actually can work with subordinates, peers, and superiors, if implemented properly. AIR stands for Action, Impact, and Result. When you approach a person, and wish to provide them feedback on performance, good or bad, you can state the Action (or behavior) you have been observing, the Impact it has on you or the team, and the Result this brings about for you, the team, or the organization. Here's an example:

"Jim, I've noticed you haven't been following all the steps for completing the assembly process (Action). This appears to have caused more errors to be found in quality inspections, and some of your co-workers think you are pulling down the team's performance measurements (Impact). This is having a negative effect on moral, and puts us at risk of sending our customers a product that doesn't meet their expectations (Result)." Now, that's a negative application, but it can also be used for positive feedback as well. Let's turn this scenario around:

"Jim, I've noticed you've been doing an excellence job in following the steps for completing the assembly process (Action). In turn, errors being found in quality inspections are down, and you've set an outstanding example for others on the team for how to do things (Impact). We've been able to ship product to our customers with a high confidence that they will get what they want and it will meet their expectations. Thank you for stepping up and setting such an outstanding example for others (Result)."

This approach to providing feedback brings the focus on the behaviors and the effect they have on the organization as a whole, keeping the big picture. It's not done in a threatening manner, but is based on observations with an outcome that the individual then can decide to change. Application of the AIR approach to feedback may be a little mechanical at first, but with practice can become a part of how you interact and communicate with your people so they can receive reinforcement of the desired changes in a manner that is palatable for even the gruffest of employees.

While implementing changes for your organization, it would be good to remember Dr. Mary Lippitt's model for managing complex change. There are five key components to that model that you'll need to maintain. Those five components are Vision, Skills, Resources, Incentives, and an Action Plan. If one of them is missing, you have a negative consequence. Below is Dr. Lippitt's model, along with the resulting negative impact of each missing component.

Managing Complex Change: *Requires 5 Components*

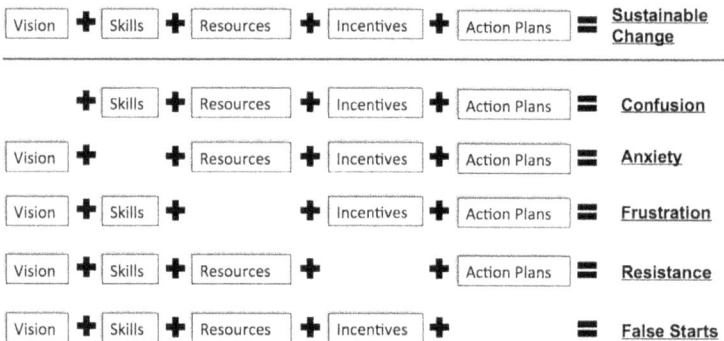

Vision	+	Skills	+	Resources	+	Incentives	+	Action Plans	=	**Sustainable Change**
	+	Skills	+	Resources	+	Incentives	+	Action Plans	=	**Confusion**
Vision	+		+	Resources	+	Incentives	+	Action Plans	=	**Anxiety**
Vision	+	Skills	+		+	Incentives	+	Action Plans	=	**Frustration**
Vision	+	Skills	+	Resources	+		+	Action Plans	=	**Resistance**
Vision	+	Skills	+	Resources	+	Incentives	+		=	**False Starts**

Note that Dr. Lippitt's model has "Vision" listed first. That's because everything starts with a vision. Just like I said that the first skill is *Establishing the Goal.* This is the compass for ensuring your organization is not only moving in the right direction, but that it is has everyone moving in the same direction.

SKILL 3: COACHING

"Mediocre people don't like high achievers, and high achievers don't like mediocre people."
— *Nick Saban*

When it comes to coaching, various things come to people's minds. If you are like me and played sports, coaching is typically envisioned as some authority figure standing around yelling at you, or blowing a whistle telling you to run laps. In business, nothing could be further from this picture (and I hope you haven't experienced the yelling version of coaching in the workplace). Coaching is about developing people to their fullest capabilities. Key to developing people is being able to communicate with them. There are certain dimensions of communication, and this information has long been available, but it's worth going over again. There are three main dimensions of communication: Verbal, Vocal, and Body/Facial expressions.

The verbal (content) aspect makes up only 7% of what is communicated to someone. In other words, what you say means less than how you say it. With that in mind, the vocal (tone) aspect makes up 38% of what's communicated. Body and Facial expressions make up a whopping 55% of what is communicated. Take away the last aspect, say you are on the phone, vocal jumps to 55%, and since 7% and 55% don't add up to 100%, that means some of the overall communication is lost.

Many people reject this off hand, but here is an example of how this works. This is especially relatable to any man who has ever been married. Take the word "fine." To the men, have you ever asked your wife, "How are you doing?," only to get the response, "Fine." The tone makes all the difference in the world in what she is saying. Add to that, body language (not looking at you, slamming things around, etc.), and maybe a frowning face. Let's face it, you are in trouble and you haven't got a clue what you've done. On the other hand, if she says, "Fine!," with a smile and upbeat tone, you know you are safe…for now. How you communicate your message is just as important as what you communicate.

Two primary responsibilities of managers/leaders are to (1) get their team to produce, and (2) develop their people. If you will focus on coaching your people, you can get both the work done and develop people at the same time. You do this, in coaching mode, by training and transferring knowledge, challenging people to improve the process, negotiating and resolving differences among your people, listening, and using questions in a way to engage people. In addition, like any good coach, when there is success you help them celebrate.

So, how do you approach your people when you need to be in a coaching mode? What kind of language/style of speaking should you use when coaching? What method of coaching should you use to drive towards Operational Excellence? These are good questions, which I'll answer right now.

There are four basic types of coaching languages: Challenging, Improving, Negotiating, and Teaching. Challenging is a coaching language directed at individuals and their performance and development. Improving is more directed at how people go about improving processes. Negotiating is for when you are dealing with people across functional lines. Teaching comes into play when you are helping individuals with the mastery of skills. All of these coaching languages can be approached using the Socratic Method. Named for the Greek philosopher Socrates, it is a form of inquiry and discussion based on asking questions of an individual, and answering, to stimulate critical thinking and stir ideas within the individual being asked questions. Open-ended questions are used to challenge the learner to think deeply. In pursuing Operational Excellence, some general questions you would ask as a coach/leader would be[3]:

1. What is the present condition in your work area? (orderly, flowing, unorganized, stilted?)
2. What is the target condition? (assuming your team has established one)
3. What is the biggest barrier or problem to achieving the target condition?
4. What is the next step we should take?
5. When can we 'go and see' what we have learned?

Below are sample questions associated with each of the four types of coaching.

Challenging: This type of language strives to produce clarification of expectations, identify deficiencies, acceptance of more difficult tasks, strategies to improve performance, and commitment to Operational Excellence. Here are some examples of the types of challenging questions you might ask:

1. How have you been performing relative to goals?
2. What is your data telling you about your performance?
3. What are your recent performance trends?
4. What are your target metrics?
5. What are the required data postings on the team board?
6. What is the commitment to the customer?
7. What is getting in the way of you being successful in meeting your goals?
8. What support do you need?
9. Do you have issues with the expectations?
10. What is your next step in making improvements?
11. When can we get together to review your next steps?
12. What have you learned from this experience?

Improving: This type of language is for process improvement conversations. The conversation should be about identifying and eliminating waste, understanding current conditions in the workplace, establishing target conditions for the workplace, and how to go about testing process improvement ideas. Some examples of improving questions include:

1. What are the metrics telling you about the possible bottleneck?

2. Can you describe the steps in the process?
3. What is happening that is an abnormality?
4. What is the trend in quality for the past two days telling you?
5. What quality checks are you doing?
6. What is the standard work process?
7. What is the standard cycle time?
8. Is there something in the process that is getting in your way?
9. Have you considered or tried any improvements?
10. Can the problem be subdivided?
11. What help do you need?
12. What can be done to avoid the reoccurrence of this problem?

Negotiating: This type of language strives to produce win-win resolutions, with differences resolved proactively, generating mutual respect, and commitment to a long-term resolution. Here are some examples of the type of questions you should ask when in a negotiating coaching mode:

1. What is the present level of cooperation?
2. What information needs to be shared?
3. What improvement is needed for understanding each other's expectations?
4. What kind of relationship is necessary to support process flow?
5. What expectations need to be established?
6. Why is it important to work collaboratively?
7. What is getting in the way of communication?
8. How can we support one another?
9. What will be done to improve the level of communication and cooperation?
10. What understanding has been reached?
11. Are commitments being met?
12. What have you learned about alliance building?

Teaching: In this type of language, you are striving to produce a focus on customers and quality, an understanding of expectations, the acquisition of skills to continually improve, a respect for the value of standardization, and mastery of the work process. Some examples of the kind of questions you'll ask are:

1. What is your understanding of the standard work?
2. What is the most difficult part of the job?
3. What training have you had on standard work?
4. Would you explain to me the standard work process?
5. What additional skills would help you be more effective in doing the standard work?
6. What are the skills needed to improve the process?
7. What support do you need to improve your skills?
8. What barriers do you face in mastering the process?
9. What is your next step to improve your skills?
10. What experienced person can you learn from?
11. What specifically do you need to know/refresh?
12. When can we get together to review your skills?

With all this discussion about talking, coaching, and asking questions, let's change gears for a moment and talk about listening. In our world today, everyone is on Facebook, Twitter, or some other type of social media, constantly posting or tweeting about their daily lives or expressing their opinion about something. Most of this is about people saying what they want to say, not listening to what others have to say. I know most of us don't believe it, or hate to admit it, but we are always talking, but not listening. For many, professionally or personally, when we talk (or tweet, or whatever), and a conversation takes place, more often than not, we are primarily interested in expressing our view, and barely listen to the other person. In fact, it's often the case that when the other person is talking, we aren't listening at all, but merely waiting our turn to start talking again. I'm willing to admit that I've caught myself in this trap on numerous occasions. Societies rarely promote listening to any serious extent. My proof? Two simple questions expose the truth:

1. How many of you have ever taken a speech class in high school or college?

2. How many of you have ever taken a class on listening?

The simple truth is that when we are taught communication skills, that training is on how to talk, not listen. It is an acquired skill, and one that can prove invaluable in connecting with the people in your organization and developing the culture of Operational Excellence. So, you think you are a good listener. Here's a test. If you answer 'yes' to three of the six following questions, you aren't as good of a listener as you might think.

1. Do you interrupt the speaker often during a conversation?
2. Do you jump to conclusions when someone is explaining a situation?
3. Do you finish other people's sentences? (how often are you wrong on what you 'finish')
4. Do you lose your temper just listening to someone?
5. Do you make up your mind about a conversation before hearing all the information?
6. Do you start forming your reply while the other person is still speaking?

I'll admit I'm guilty of all of these at one time or another. Knowing I'm not perfect, the key is minimizing how often I do these things. We can all be better listeners if we'll focus on eliminating these negative attributes from our communications. Work on being an active listener. When someone is talking, hear what they are actually saying, focus on that, not what you want to say next. Search for the real meaning in their message (remember the different dimensions of communication?). If someone is agitated and complaining, it may not be the topic at hand that really has them upset, but something else that has made them generally grumpy. That leads to listening for the feeling and meaning of their message, and then you can evaluate the message to understand what they are trying to get at.

Once you've done these things, then you can respond to the message in a thoughtful manner. Don't forget your Socratic approach, which might be good at this point, depending on what they said. Before issuing an answer or definitive reply, if there is any question concerning what they are getting at, you can clarify with a simple reply: "So, what I am hearing you say is...(and repeat back to them what you think they said)." You'll either get confirmation, or clarification. From there you can move forward with a sound response, and you will have gained respect from the person you are conversing with because they will be grateful you actually listened to what they had to say, and you responded appropriately.

Beyond just talking and listening, coaching includes showing a person how to do something. The Japanese term for this is 'Shu Ha Ri,' and can be loosely translated 'Learn, Do, Coach.' This is a systematic cycle of teaching with three distinct stages of learning: you start with basic knowledge, then separate skills are mastered and linked together, and finally repetition of these skills to practice until mastered as a whole.

In coaching the learner, the coach will first do the particular process while the student watches. Then the student will try to emulate the process as demonstrated, with feedback from the coach. Next, the coach will go through the process, verbalizing the steps in the process as they do them, then the student again goes through the process and verbalizes the steps, like the coach did. Again, the coach will do the process; verbalize the steps, with additional key points added in and the importance of each step. The student will repeat all of this for the coach. From here, the student practices the steps, talking themselves through the process, and does this over and over until it is automatic for them.

During all of this, the coach is still responsible for the actions of the student, and should give feedback as required (with the assumption that over time less and less feedback will be required). Finally, the student should get to the point where they can do the process without having to think about every step. At this point, the student will have mastered the process to the point where they will be allowed to analyze and improve upon the process and make the improvements part of the new standard work. From here, the student is now ready to be a coach and train others in the process. Of course, the amount of time this will take, for the student to master the process and become a coach, depends on the complexity of the process and the attention they get from their coach.

Whether coaching an individual or a team, you want to ensure that you have your current process condition well documented, and you have talked with the team about what the future/target condition should look like that you are shooting for. Yes, there will be obstacles, known and unknown, but if you have clear, specific metrics (such as lead time, output per hour, inventory level, quality level, etc.), you can set your target and track your performance in reaching that future state. Use the various coaching skills provided here in guiding your people to mastery and independence in reaching that future state.

Remember, grasp the current situation. As you and your people go through the process of improving things, learning is just as important as the improvement you seek itself. Part of the goal here is to develop your people for the long term, not just for the short term fix. You want to create a cadre of problem solvers! Here are some things you want to instill in your people that will help in your pursuit of Operational Excellence:

1. Always chase perfection.

2. Create a standard for how you want to do things.

3. Everybody needs to buy into that standard or you lose team chemistry.

4. Get everyone focused on doing their job to the highest level every time and success will come.

5. Everyone should take pride in their performance and doing things right all the time; this becomes the culture and drives how people think about their work.

6. Invest in excellence (your people, your equipment, and your facility).

7. Always be evaluating your people, and do so thoroughly.

These seven items remind me of a time I was working with a facility and helping them improve their processes to increase their quality and volume of output. They weren't ready to embrace the full concept of Operational Excellence, but they were willing to try implementing some changes. The facility was basically a large fabrication shop, and one of the items they made was large tanks for holding fluids. There were various steps in the flow of making the tanks, from rolling sheet metal for sections of the walls, to creating tops and bottoms for the tanks. Each step was done in a different location, and they were done in batches not tied to any job, or tied to a shift (and therefore not to any particular worker). By the time Quality inspected the tank and found issues, there was no way of clearly identifying where exactly the flaw had originated, or who had been involved in the poor quality. This led to a lot of rework, driving up costs, and the organization was at a loss as to how to identify the root cause. Once we had documented the process, and identified potential areas for improvement, the improvement team came up with a unique, even radical, approach to working on the tanks. Since people worked at stations and only made tops, or bottoms, or coiled sheet metal, or welded the coils together to make the walls, they didn't have a full picture of the impact they had on the final project. The improvement team decided to create small production teams of six people each that took a particular job (tied to an order), and worked together from beginning to end of the process to produce a tank. This meant they coiled the sheet metal together, made the tops and bottoms together, and welded everything into a tank together. They had ownership of that tank. I called this a 'moving cell' because we couldn't move all the equipment to centrally locate it for them to do all their work in one place, but instead they followed the path through the facility from station to station for each process as a group.

SKILL 4: EMPOWERING

"As we look into the next century, leaders will be those
who empower others."
— Bill Gates

The first time I can recall hearing the term 'empowering' was during a speech from a Brigadier General that I was under the command of when I was in the U.S. Air Force. It was both inspiring and enlightening. Here was a commander who wanted to push decision making, as he said, "Down to the lowest level possible." Based on my experiences in the Air Force, I thought this a radical idea, and one that was fantastic. Once I left the Air Force, I discovered in multiple civilian organizations this was a radical idea as well. Now, decades later, even with all the books out there on continuous improvement and how to be a leader, there are a lot of organizations where this is still a radical idea.

The fact that so many supervisors, managers, and senior management seem to want to hold onto the decision making process for themselves appears to me to be an indicator of one of several possibilities. First, they are control freaks and derive their power base from the ability to be the sole decision maker. Second, perhaps they fear letting others make decisions because they think it might make them look weak, or appear to not know the answer (and the boss should always have the answer, in their mind). Finally, and what is often the case, they were taught, formally or by example, that only the boss makes decisions, and allowing those below you to have a say isn't how things are done.

From the moment I heard that General speak about empowerment, it freed me from the concept that as an officer I had to know everything and make all the decisions. I realized that I had a wealth of knowledge at my fingertips in the form of the men and women that reported to me. I didn't need to know everything, but I did need to know which of my people had the information I needed, and what the status of things was within the organization. With that in mind, let's clarify what empowerment is:

Empowerment is based on the idea that giving employees skills, resources, authority, opportunity, and motivation, as well as holding them responsible and accountable for outcomes of their actions, will contribute to their competence and satisfaction in their work environment.

By empowering your people, you, as the leader, demonstrate support and commitment to a culture of Operational Excellence. In order to cultivate this kind of culture, it is imperative that you delegate responsibility and decision making, and that there are clear boundaries for these areas with principles and processes in place to help your people make decisions. Be sure and establish expectations for individuals as well as for teams, with regular follow up to establish the commitment to these ideals. Leaders need to always be encouraging their people to pursue problem solving and coming up with ideas for issues related to their areas and the business as a whole. You must also work on developing the capabilities of your people.

When promoting the empowerment of your people, there are certain "engagement drivers" that you will want to use, known as the 3 C's.[4] These are Connection, Control, and Creativity.

Connection: Base your empowerment around results. Have your employees work as a team and provide input into goal setting for the team. Make sure those goals have metrics that are specifically tied to them, and that these metrics are posted for all to see, and are kept updated. Provide opportunities for the team to interact with their customer (even if it's internal customers) so that they understand their needs.

Control: Make sure your employees' empowerment is tied to the processes they interact with and/or are responsible for. You want them to understand the current state, and know what future state they are striving for. Allow them to have the ability to stop the process for quality issues so those issues can be addressed and they can get moving again. Make support resources readily available to them, and that team members are engaged in improvement events. Develop your people so they are problem solvers and can feel comfortable tackling issues. Introduce them to preventative maintenance and the concept of Total Productive Maintenance (TPM).

Note: You might run into the issue of people claiming they don't have time to participate in all this "problem solving stuff." That's old school thinking, and pushback on the culture change that is happening. Simply put, they need to make time. Look, if you are in a hurry on your way to work, and you get a flat tire, you don't have time for it do you? No, but you have to take care of it. Same thing with work processes. We don't have time to fix things, but they will eventually break down, and then we are in a real mess. Better to fix things as you go along, rather than waiting for a catastrophic failure that puts your business at risk.

Creativity: This is where you want to promote personal development, and allow people to try new things. Experimentation, within defined boundaries, is a good thing, and encourages creative thinking among your team, and thus you are headed down the path to creating a team of problem solvers. Be sure and cross train your people. Not only does this provide flexibility in your workforce, but enhances their perspectives on how processes are done. Challenge your people's thought processes and knowledge. Set stretch goals for them and provide increasingly difficult tasks for them to accomplish. Exercising the mind is just as important as exercising the body.

Tools for Empowerment

When looking to empower your team, be sure and make clear what exactly they are empowered to do. You need to have clearly defined goals and expectations when asking them to take the initiative and allowing them to make decisions and take action without always checking with you first. It would also be good to have some kind of suggestion program or "idea system." These kinds of programs have been around for a long time, and often fail due to lack of management action on suggested improvements.

For a program like this to work, there needs to be a clear, simple process for submitting ideas, a process for reviewing the ideas (maybe a committee with members that rotate on and off the committee), the ideas are reviewed quickly, with appropriate feedback to those submitting the ideas whether the idea will be implemented or not, and if not, why. In addition, you need to have some kind of formal recognition for those ideas implemented, whether a reward system, or just public expressions of appreciation. Then the ideas need to be implemented as soon as feasible so people feel like their input matters.

You want your people to be flexible, not only in their thinking, but in their abilities. This allows for the organization to respond as required to changing events in your field of work. You need to cross train your people so that resources can be shifted as needed depending on volumes of orders, or influx of customers, again depending on the type of business you are in. If you don't have skills flexibility among your people, you risk being limited in your response times to customer demands. You need to keep some kind of chart that you can track the skills your people know, and to what level of competency they have mastered the various skills. This not only helps in knowing who is available to fill in when demands change, but also lets you know where you need to focus in continuing to develop your people.

Every improvement effort should be handled in a structured, disciplined way so you avoid "mission creep" and the project doesn't get dropped or pushed aside due to the latest crisis. I recommend using the A3 charter form to track your projects. This is a simple but effective tool for establishing a charter for your improvement efforts, and allows team members to clearly know what they are doing, what are the expectations of them, and what are the expected results. An A3 charter will typically look something like this:

CHARTER	
Project Name: Downhole Distribution "Receiving Area" Kaizen Problem Statement/Business Case: Improve accuracy and timeliness of Receiving, Inspecting, Stocking and Pulling parts Goal Statement: 1) Identify potential areas for improvement in processes for receiving, inspecting, stocking, pulling parts. 2) Develop process flow documents that can be used for cross-training and increase visibility of tasks performed between different groups	Team Composition: Sponsor: Chris L.. Process Owner: Jay G. Project Leaders: Ron C., Dan P. Team: Randy K. Donna W. Simon M. Erika B.
Established CTQ's ("Critical to Quality" Measures): • Cycle Time for receiving, inspecting, stocking and pulling parts • % Part not found • % Complete and Accurate stocking and pulling of parts Within Scope: • Processes for Downhole Distribution's parts received, inspected, stocked and pulled for shipment • Facility layout for receiving, inspecting, stocking and pulling of parts Out of Scope: Packing and Shipping of parts	Project Kickoff Date: 8/13/20XX Estimated End Date: 8/24/20XX Expected Deliverables: • Identification of potential areas for improvement of communication, and accuracy and timeliness of deliverables between key processes • Timeline for updated and clear Work Instructions & SOPs • Identification of most efficient and effective facility layout • Identification of how to optimize JDE and RF tracking • Potential quick-wins Expected Benefit (Description): • Improved quality and timely delivery of parts • Improved visibility and communication between groups • Standardization of processes, SOPs Work Instructions • Plans for optimization of JDE and RF tracking

Rather than going into detail about how to fill in the form, I've provided an outline that asks questions in each section that you will need to answer. Do this, and you'll have established a good, simple charter to keep your improvement efforts on track:

CHARTER	
Project Name: What Process will be examined or redesigned? **Problem Statement/Business Case:** Why are we doing this project? What problem are we solving? Why is it important? What difference will it make? **Goal Statement:** What improvement are we targeting and what will be the impact on performance?	**Team Composition:** **Sponsor:** **Process Owner:** **Project Leaders:** **Team Members:** Consider who needs to be on this team for our project to be successful? Who are the key people and major players that will impact the project and be impacted BY the project? Will the sponsor be able to commit the time, people, and other resources needed?
Established Measures: What metrics exist for us to measure current and future state of the process? (These should be something that matters and benefits the ultimate customer.)	**Project Kickoff Date:** When are we starting the project? **Estimated End Date:** When are we committing to finish it?
Within Scope: What are the boundaries of the project? What areas or items will be investigated by our team? What resources will be provided in terms of time, equipment, and money to make this happen?	**Expected Deliverables:** What are the outcomes that we will produce and by when? When will key milestones be reached? What Continuous Improvement tools will we use to carry out the project?
Out of Scope: What processes, products, or issues are outside of the project? What is "out of bounds" and will not be looked at?	**Expected Benefit (Description):** What is the expected benefit in terms of $ saved, time saved, lead and/or cycle time improvements, inventory reduction, etc. What are specific measurable outcomes – what are the metrics and measures? How will the project results be measured, and by whom? Who from outside the project (i.e. Finance) be able to measure and verify success?

Remember when filling out the charter that your outcomes need to fit the SMART acronym:

Specific, Measurable, Achievable, Relevant, Timely

Make things visible. Visual management is a key tool that helps when empowering your people. You have areas you are measuring on your journey to Operational Excellence. Put up a board in each work area where the measurements/metrics you are tracking for that area are posted. By making things visible, people will be more aware of how they are doing. In addition, have your people keep the board updated; empower them to control the tracking and updating of the metrics so they have ownership of their processes and how they are doing.

Conduct stand-up meetings. This is a powerful tool to get your team on the same page, and eliminate problems before they ever begin. First, let's put an emphasis on "stand-up." Don't go to a conference room or office and have everyone sit down. You'll never get out of there. Conduct the meeting in the work place, and everyone stands up in a circle and you cover a structured format for conducting the meeting. These aren't intended to be half-hour long conversations where people air complaints, they are short meetings, five to ten minutes in which you hit some highlights and key notices before everyone gets to work. Daily stand-up meetings help everyone get focused at the beginning of every shift/work day. Focus on answering a few key questions for the day: What did you do yesterday? What is scheduled for today? Are there any issues you see that are barriers to doing your work?

From here, if time permits, you might make a few announcements, but the idea is to make sure yesterday went well, everyone knows what they need to do today. Are they on track or not (ahead of schedule or behind schedule), what might be causing them problems in being successful today? Tackling these issues is part of the day's work, not the stand-up meeting. If it's a recurring issue, then maybe you set up a team and form a charter to tackle the problem, but the team does it, not management. Leading often requires letting go.

SKILL 5: COLLABORATING

*"If everyone is moving forward together,
then success takes care of itself."*
— *Henry Ford*

What does it really mean when people talk about collaborating? In business terms, it means that your team and/or organization has a strong commitment to jointly achieving clearly stated objectives, and does this by sharing knowledge, learning from one another, and building consensus. Team members should understand and appreciate the functions of other team members, and work to align their activities with one another, leveraging their collective efforts to meet their shared goals. In addition, everyone has established performance expectations with customers and suppliers, and work to hold each other accountable.

Remember Kevin Duggan's definition of Operational Excellence? "Each and every employee can see the flow of value to the customer and fix that flow before it breaks down."[1] Collaboration supports this vision of Operational Excellence when there is close coordination of functions to serve the value stream. This means that a high performing team cannot afford breakdowns in communication, and therefore the interdependency between processes in the value stream is at a high level. With proper collaboration, you can maximize your resources and have the quick, integrated responses that are essential for your high performing team.

Unless you are already part of a high functioning team, you will have to build collaboration among the various functions of your organization.

Start by looking at the informal relationships among your people. If they are strong, great, if not, then you will need to start fostering these relationships. Are there formal structures and practices in place? Are these structures and practices conducive to continuous improvement and Operational Excellence? If not, you will need to overhaul them. If they aren't in place now, then you can implement them with your goal in mind. Make sure you have clarification of everyone's role, and how it impacts the overall strategy of the organization. Take time to do some team building. This can be done at work or away from the work environment. You, as the leader, should know your people and what might appeal to them for this effort. If you don't know, then start asking your people questions, or set up a small committee to help develop some team building opportunities.

For the informal relationship building, as the leader you should work on engaging in one-on-one conversations; get to know your people better. Have some informal meetings where you can discuss their concerns. This can be during a break, over coffee, or during lunch. Looking at your formal structures and practices, take time to walk the floor with people and see what is happening in the workplace. Make sure your subject matter experts are visible in the workplace; consider co-locating functions within the value stream to enhance communication. Establish a steering committee to help drive your strategy, and set up some value stream project teams across functional lines.

Make sure that when you are clarifying roles that this is done in alignment with your shared strategic goals, and support the activity of the value stream. Once this is done, be sure and take time to recognize those individuals and teams that are actively supporting those goals. In addition, you will want to incorporate the contributions of people to the value stream and goals in performance plans and performance reviews.

Make sure and collaborate with your customers and suppliers as well. Too often people want to keep things secret. What better way to meet the needs of your customers, and have your suppliers meet your needs than to share with them, as much as possible, your plans and goals, and how working together you can help one another meet all your plans and goals. Consider doing some joint planning with key suppliers and customers. This can help improve the flow of activity among your businesses. When possible, consider co-locating staff so they can provide better information and support. Develop informal relationships between your organization and suppliers and customers. People will open up about their needs and concerns if they feel they have a meaningful relationship with you. Let your suppliers know you are striving for Operational Excellence, and offer to train them on continuous improvement methodologies if they are not already familiar with them. Help improve how their business flows, because it helps your business flow better. This is a win-win. Take joint visits to one another's facilities and get a fresh set of eyes on what is going on, seeing how things might be handled better. When new products are being developed, it's a good idea to get both suppliers and customers involved early on to minimize issues that could crop up later.

Within your own organization, ensure that you have cross functional collaboration by instituting joint floor walks, where people from various functions go together and observe the various work places, looking for opportunities to improve things. Remember the stand-up meetings? Occasionally conduct joint stand-up meetings between groups that feed or support one another in the value stream. When possible, consider co-locating staff in the workplace (such as putting your engineers on the floor where operations can interact with them regularly without there being a major effort for them to get together). Try letting the internal customers provide feedback that can be used in performance evaluations. This helps people better understand the implications of their actions within the organization. Make sure that when developing plans and strategies that there is validation across functional lines so, again, everyone is supporting the over-arching goals of the organization, and not working at self-serving cross purposes.

That last item leads into more team collaboration. As you go forward with these plans, and they enhance the performance of the overall organization, leadership needs to be sure and be visible in the workplace. This helps with knowing if knowledge is being properly transferred among teams, and they are learning to support one another. When this takes place, good things begin to happen, and that provides an opportunity to celebrate successes. As mentioned before, take time to recognize individual and group successes. No matter how big or small, acknowledge when things are done the right way, or have a positive impact. This positive reinforcement will promote more of the same actions in the future.

Take a moment here and think about everything I just said. Use this and evaluate the current state of collaboration within your organization. In conducting this evaluation, ask yourself these questions:

1. What are the informal relationships like in my organization?
2. How often, if ever, do I engage employees in one-on-one conversations? How far down in the organization do I go when I have these conversations?
3. Do I ever discuss concerns informally with team members?
4. How often do I go on workplace walks? Do I do them with other team members?
5. Does our organization have clearly defined, shared goals that everyone is aware of and understand? Are these shared goals aligned around the value stream?
6. Can I observe cross-functional collaboration?
7. Do all the teams conduct daily stand-up meetings? How effective are they?
8. Is there evidence that knowledge is being transferred?
9. How often do we celebrate successes, if at all? How do we celebrate them?

I mentioned earlier, in the *Defining Operational Excellence and Leadership* section, that leadership can be situational. When collaborating with others, understanding how to adjust your leadership style is vital to being able to connect with others. It is a fairly common practice today for organizations to have their people take tests to know and understand their 'social style' or 'behavior style.' There are a number of these tests [5], and they all use different terminology for the different styles, but there are usually four of them. For our purposes here, I'm going to define these four styles with the terms I have used most recently. But before providing the terms and definitions, I'll review the concept a little for those that are not familiar with this kind of test.

The basic principle behind the social style test is that there are four social styles, and everyone falls into one of the four. The concept is social styles focus on observable behavior, not personality, which goes much deeper. Behavior can be modified by conscious choice, whereas the personality cannot be. The goal in understanding the social styles is so you can be more effective with others through understanding your style and theirs, and how they relate/interact. You don't need to change who you are, but modify what you do when interacting with others. The goal in studying the social styles is to understand them and increase your flexibility in your interaction with others.

As I said, there are four basic social styles. Everyone has a dominant style that influences the way they behave at work (and at home too, but it can be totally different depending on the environment. We are focused here on the work environment). Of the four social styles, none are better or worse, they just influence your interaction with others. Most studies suggest that among all populations people are evenly distributed among the four styles.

The four social styles run along two continuums: Results oriented and Emotions oriented. The results continuum extends from process oriented (very methodical, routine oriented) to expedience oriented (quick acting, likes change). The emotions continuum extends from control oriented (formal, self-controlled) to responsive oriented (animated, engaging). From these two continuums, we get the four social styles: Analytical, Amiable, Driver, and Expressive. The four styles, and their traits, are shown on the chart on the next page:

Social Style Quadrants

(Controlled)

(Process)	**Analytical** Organized Detailed Logical Consistent Precise - Facts & Details (Get all the information)	**Driver** Direct Independent Swift Determined Decisive - Action & Results (Make a decision)	**(Expedience)**
	Amiable Cooperative Patient Supportive Friendly/Warm Easy Going - Harmony & Security (Work as a team)	**Expressive** Enthusiastic Animated Creative Stimulating Quick Decisions - Spontaneity & New Ideas (Have fun)	

(Responsive)

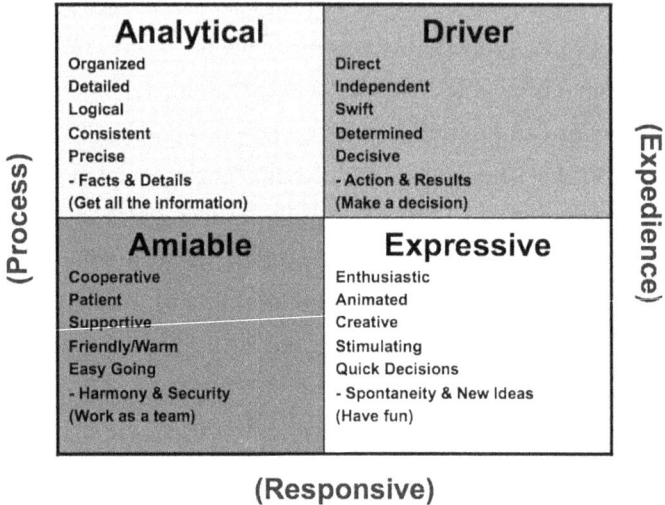

Not only is it important to know and understand your social style, but know and understand the social style of people you interact with. If you want to collaborate with people, it is best to approach them in a way that meets their needs and is appealing to them. For example, if an Analytical person is going to approach an Expressive, rather than walk in with a lot of details and get right to the point and start analyzing things, meet the Expressive where they are. Ask them how their weekend was, and take time for their occasional brainstorming creative views they feel the need to share. Patience is a virtue. Personally, I'm a Driver and I like to do things quickly with just a few options to pick from so I can get to work and knock things out. This can drive the other styles crazy, so I have to make sure if I'm approaching an Analytical that I have the facts and data together, and give them time to absorb the information before talking about what needs to be done. And I need to let them share their thoughts, no matter how long it takes them to do it, so they are on board with whatever decision is made.

I have a simple way I keep the four social styles in mind, and relatable to me, that expresses each one:

Analytical – "Let's do it the right way."

Driver – "Let's do it my way."

Expressive – "Let's do it the fun way."

Amiable – "Let's do it whichever way, as long as we all get along."

I want to stress again that these are social/behavior styles, and they are about how you interact with people, and your needs and communication style (in this case concerning the work environment). They aren't necessarily who you are or define everything about you.

At one company I worked for, I had a boss who was very intelligent and an extreme Analytical (to a Driver like me, this could get really annoying). When our company started taking the social styles classes, everyone took the test and then we went around announcing what our social style was. My boss became irate when it was discovered that not everyone was an Analytical. Somehow he had missed the point of the exercise and was of the mind that you had to analyze information in business, and therefore how could you not be an Analytical and expect to function in the work place. He argued for a while with the instructor over this, but finally let it go and was most disappointed that so many of his co-workers were not Analytical. Instead of learning from the process how to better engage his co-workers, my boss lost respect for them. I was actually very surprised at his lack of flexibility.

Over the years of teaching the social styles myself, I've found that all four share one trait: Everyone wants to be shown respect. You can do that by approaching people in a manner that plays to their social style. And remember, no one style is better than the others. Leaders come from each of the four styles. I would suggest that you have your organization take one of the social style tests out there, have people proudly post at their desk or work station which of the four they are, and start using this information to help people interact more effectively in their collaboration. This will take time, but anything worth doing takes effort. Below are a couple of charts on versatility that can help your team members determine how to best interact with one another and meet people where they are at so they can foster effective collaboration.

Prescriptions for Versatility

	Amiable	Analytical	Driver	Expressive
Needs to Know about:	How it will affect their personal circumstances	How they can justify it logically / how it works	What it does / by when / what it costs	How it enhances their status and visibility
Do it:	Friendly	Precisely	Rapidly	Dynamically
Save them:	Conflict	Embarrassment	Time	Effort
To facilitate decision making, provide:	Personal service & assurances	Data & documentation	Options with supporting analysis	Testimonials & incentives
Likes you to be:	Pleasant	Precise	To the point	Stimulating
Support their:	Feelings	Procedures	Goals	Ideas

Prescriptions for Versatility

	Amiable	Analytical	Driver	Expressive
Create this environment:	Personal	Serious	Businesslike	Enthusiastic
Maintain this pace:	Slow / Relaxed	Slow / Systematic	Fast / Decisive	Fast / spontaneous
Focus on this priority:	The relationship / Communication	The task / The process	The task / The result	The relationship / Interaction
At play be:	Casual and cooperative	Structured / Play by the rules	Competitive & aggressive	Spontaneous & playful
Use time to:	Develop the relationship	Ensure accuracy	Act efficiently	Enjoy the interaction
Write this way:	Warm & friendly	Detailed & precise	Short & to the point	Informal & dramatic
On the telephone be:	Warm & pleasant	Businesslike & precise	Short & to the point	Conversational & playful

Leverage this knowledge to build teams and get buy in to the organizational goals. When you approach an individual in a manner that connects with their social style, they are much more likely to be open to collaborating and looking at the bigger picture of Operational Excellence. Keep the end goal in mind. Which is more important: Getting things your way, or helping the team/organization achieve its overall goals and everyone being successful?

SKILL 6: ACCOUNTABILITY

"Accountability separates the wishers in life from the action-takers that care enough about their future to account for their daily actions."
— *John Di Lemme*

It seems that in some organizations, the word "accountability" is an ugly term. In these types of organizations, accountability is to be avoided at all costs. People in these organizations want to avoid responsibility because the word has a negative connotation to it due to how leadership reacts when they identify "accountable" people. The fact is, high performing organizations embrace accountability, and consider it an honor to be accountable. It isn't an opportunity to blame someone, but an opportunity for learning and improving on how they do things. In addition, being accountable helps us to be responsible and prevents us from being "victims."

When people play the victim, there are certain stages they will go through to avoid being accountable. I'm sure these will sound familiar to many of you reading this. When there's an issue, rather than be accountable, people will often point fingers at others, or declare "It's not my job." Sometimes people will try to ignore the issue, or worse, deny that an issue even exists (until things really blow up, and then out comes the finger pointing). Sometimes people claim ignorance, and in a command and control environment that isn't on the path to continuous improvement or Operational Excellence, they wait for someone to tell them what to do, rather than take the initiative and "own" the issue and solve it. Others will do a CYA (Cover Your Ass) action so they can claim innocence. One of the toughest stances is those who take a wait and see position. These people will want to claim innocence too, but if you are in the process of striving to drive your organization towards Operational Excellence, the wait and see people fall into the "lukewarm allies" of Machiavelli's quote in the *Handling Change* section.

So, how do we instill accountability in our organization?

Several things need to take place, some of which I've mentioned earlier in this book. Work with your team and come up with a few critical metrics that will have a positive impact on your performance. Using the visual management concept, post these metrics on the team board for all to see. Give ownership to the team leader to keep these metrics updated. Maybe even rotate the responsibility for updating the metrics among group members so they all feel ownership of keeping them current. Metrics should be reviewed at the stand-up meetings, which I will assume you will have put in place. Leadership should follow up on these actions during their regular walk arounds, and address any short comings (metrics not updated, missing targets, etc.), but remember this should be done using techniques from the *Coaching* section. Finally, team members should be working together towards the common goals, so they should be holding one another accountable (remember my story of the tank fabrication teams in the *Coaching* section?).

When implementing the accountability factor in to your culture of Operational Excellence, there are several principles you need to keep in mind:

1. No hiding behind titles, silos, or excuses. People need to "own" the process or situation, especially if you are the leader. You can't decide that as the "boss" you are going to delegate accountability. Everyone has to be accountable. Silos, that's old school thinking. In Operational Excellence, there is flow, and everyone one is a part of the entire value stream, so no finger pointing, but instead search for the root cause, which does not point to a person, but an issue with a process. There may be explanations, but no excuses. You cannot be the victim of situations. Quite frankly, in my experience

I've found Sales to be the biggest victims, yet they want to say they drive the business. They can't have it both ways. In his book, "Continuous Permanent Improvement," Arun Hariharan talks about Sales and doing things First Time Right (FTR)[6]. In short, Hariharan removes the excuses Sales often use for stating why they can't do process improvement, or be a part of Operational Excellence. In a more traditional, reactive organization, Sales personnel claim they are at the mercy of the customer's whims, and can't do anything to change or improve their processes. They think they have to react to the customer. In truth, if they were truly listening to the voice of the customer, Sales personnel would be proactive and improve their processes so they wouldn't be waiting to act on customer complaints, but be forward thinking and start to anticipate the needs of their customers.

2. Your SME's (Subject Matter Experts) and specialists (especially your continuous improvement people) are accountable to operations. They have to be available and willing to provide support to operations to help meet the team goals.

3. Your people should not interact and make decisions based on "war stories" and anecdotal information. They should speak with data, so sound decisions are being made that can be properly measured based on the metrics the teams have chosen to track their performance.

4. People need to be open and honest, respecting one another's input and opinion. Without this, you will limit if not completely shut down communication and the sharing of knowledge, and thus prevent your organization from reaching its full potential as a high performing team.

5. Leaders should be able to facilitate constructive conflict. Sometimes an issue comes up either in a stand-up meeting or other type of meeting that is not pertinent to the meeting at hand, or is too complicated to settle in the time available. These issues need to be taken off line, or in other words, tabled with a time set for a later date to get back together to resolve the matter. Too often I've seen

half hour meetings drag out two hours or more because people are dickering over something irrelevant to the meeting at hand. In some cases, the 30 minutes get eaten up with opinion rather than substance, and by having to stick to a strict time limit the meeting ends with nothing accomplished. Accountability matters in meetings as well.

Let's review some accountability tools that are readily available to you. Some have been mentioned already, but reviewing doesn't hurt. The daily stand-up meeting has been discussed at length already, but as an accountability tool, it provides a time for touching on what's been accomplished, if someone hasn't accomplished their responsibilities, then ask why. Not to punish, but as an opportunity to eliminate barriers and challenge the person to be innovative and think differently about how to solve things (not work around them). Walking the floor provides a good opportunity to see what people are doing, and if they are being accountable for what is happening in their area. It's a good time to check the metrics board; see if they are owning the process and keeping the board updated. Also, set regular performance reviews (not just the formal annual feedback that's documented for HR), identifying strengths and areas for improvement in how they are embracing Operational Excellence.

In commenting about walking the floor, it reminds me of one plant manager I knew that took great pride in making a daily walk through the entire plant he was responsible for. He liked to say that every morning he got up from his desk went through every area of the facility; that he liked to keep in touch with the work that was going on and keep his hands "a little dirty." Every day, like clockwork, he started his walk at 7:30am. He took the same path through the plant, every day, and everyone knew when he was going to be coming by their area. The thing is, this plant manager methodically walked the plant every day. He walked non-stop, with his head down, never stopping to talk to people or enquire as to what was happing, how things were going, or if there were any issues he could help solve. He didn't even acknowledge you when he went by. I saw people say, "Hi," or "Morning," and he just kept walking with his head down, never hearing anyone.

I experienced this for myself one time. I was on the shop floor, dealing with changing the flow of a particular department when the plant manager walked by. He walked by so close he almost ran into me. I wanted to show him what I was doing and get his feedback, so I called his name and started to ask him about the change to the layout, but he kept walking with his head down, never acknowledging me. The employees in the area started laughing, and it was as much at me for trying to talk to the plant manager as it was for him walking on by. The employees had a term for the plant manager's daily walks. They called it "hunting for dimes," because it looked like he was walking along looking for loose change on the ground, too engrossed in his search to see what was happening around him. Accountability was not a part of the culture of this facility.

Ultimately, accountability is about instilling in the members of your organization the desire to take ownership of their situation and determine how to overcome obstacles and achieve the established goals. There have been many times in my life where things have not gone as I thought they should, or wished, and have had to step back and ask myself, "Okay, given that I'm in this situation, due to these events, what do I do now?" Some people find lots of excuses and blame others. Some people get angry, lash out, and make their situation worse. Still, others simply fold; they quit trying.

Life goes on. Quitting isn't a sound option. To achieve excellence, you have to ask questions, be self-reflective. Some of the questions you should ask:

1. How did this happen? (answer honestly)
2. How did I contribute to this?
3. What can I learn from this so it doesn't happen again?
4. What can I do to fix this, if it is fixable?
5. Who can I turn to for advice or assistance?
6. Where do I go from here?
7. What is my next step forward?
8. What else can I do to overcome this situation and achieve my goal/target condition?

Within an organization, there must be accountability for results. It is required to achieve Operational Excellence. Without accountability, you will miss out on innovation, customer satisfaction, high performing teams, and there will be no development of your people to create high performing teams. Everyone must remember there is one problem: everyone's problem. With accountability, the team will solve it together.

While bringing about a culture of accountability and moving your organization towards Operational Excellence, remember that there will be a number of things that will threaten establishing this new culture. Some of these are:

1. Entitlement – Under the old system, certain people feel they have a right to certain positions, treatment, or aren't responsible for certain things. They will resist the new system of ownership and accountability. This will have to be dealt with immediately, coaching them through to seeing the new way, and why the new way is best for all. There is also the entitlement mindset of millennials and younger people. This is a different type of entitlement. They want it all now, and they want their independence to make decisions and do things their way. Rather than trying to "put them in their place," play off of these desires to help usher in change, and ownership of the processes.

2. Poor performance (lack of feedback) – People don't necessarily know they are failing to do the right things unless you tell them. Coaching techniques come in very handy here to keep things positive. Also remember the AIR (Action, Impact, Result) technique mentioned in the Coaching section. Constant feedback, positive and re-directive, are necessary to promote a high performing team.

3. Misalignment – If people don't know where they are supposed to be headed, how can they be accountable? Everyone needs to know what the strategic goals are, and what their role is in achieving those goals. Leadership needs to lead! Let people know what the true expectations are, and if the expectations change, let them know that too.

4. Poor communication – This one connects with numbers 2 and 3

above. Remember, you manage things, you lead people. Managers don't talk to their people, but leaders do. Engage your people and let them know what's going on. Your team needs to be informed to the level they need to take knowledgeable action. Make sure they have what they need, information wise, to be successful. Don't keep everything a secret, and then criticize people for their actions.

5. Lack of people development – Too often I've seen how managers resist training their people. This has always baffled me. Whenever I've advocated improving the skills of people, managers usually say something to the effect, "If we do that, they'll just go somewhere else and make more money." Am I the only one that sees something wrong with that logic? It almost sounds as if these managers want a staff of poorly trained people. Members of your organization will leave out of frustration if you don't develop them. Investing in your people shows you care, gives you better performing employees, and develops a level of loyalty to you and your organization as you all succeed together.

6. Lack of empowerment – If managers don't let go of the command and control mentality and become leaders of people who are free to act and make things better, you will lose. Both your people and to your competitors. This may seem scary to some managers, but if you communicate with your people, develop them and empower them, it will be liberating for you and your team.

SKILL 7: MENTORING

"The delicate balance of mentoring someone is not creating them in your own image, but giving them the opportunity to create themselves."
— *Steven Spielberg*

I've seen the term "mentor" used in a number of places, and the meaning behind this term is not always the same. The understanding of what a mentor is has ranged from someone who is tagged with the title (sometimes resentfully, which creates a terrible situation for the mentee), to people who volunteer to mentor others willingly. Whether compelled to "mentor," or they volunteer, most people's intentions are sincere. However, sometimes people confuse the term "gofer" with "mentee," and treat the mentee as an administrative assistant rather than a future leader they are helping to develop. However, some people actually try to be a true mentor, but more often than not, those that assigned them as mentors simply assume they know what to do. This isn't necessarily always the case. So we need to ask, and answer, several questions about mentoring.

What is mentoring really? Simply put, mentoring is a relationship between a more experienced individual and a less experienced individual. It's a two-way relationship, meaning that there is give and take, questions and answers, coaching and receiving of coaching, between the experienced and less experienced individuals. The key objective is to help develop the less experienced person's skills, abilities, and knowledge so they can grow in their duties and prepare them for more rigorous opportunities. A benefit of this relationship is that the more experienced member of the mentoring relationship is challenged by the experience to refine and enhance their knowledge and abilities, and improve on their skills of teaching/coaching others. For the organization as a whole, this enhances both parties' abilities, enhances the organization's people, and potentially helps with succession planning.

Who should be a mentor? Mentors should not just be volunteers. I've seen mentoring programs where the organization allowed anyone above a certain level to volunteer, and there was no screening process or training for these soon to be mentors. Some of them were fine, while others were models of the worst aspects of the organization. The latter individuals simply perpetuated those negative traits, passing them on to their mentees. Even worse, the mentees can be turned off to the mentoring program, and leave them disillusioned about the company. This can drive off good employees, costing the company young talent. Ideally, mentors are experienced individuals who have demonstrated skills in being coaches, teachers, or counselors, and are known for their patience and wisdom. Without an adequate number of such individuals, your organization needs to have a program to train the potential mentors on how to properly handle the mentoring role. If there is no formal mentoring program, and an individual is seeking out a mentor on their own, they must look for a role model they believe will challenge them and bring out the best in them, while demonstrating the kind of leadership attributes discussed in earlier sections of this book.

How does the mentoring relationship work? The role of the mentee is to learn, and the role of the mentor is to teach. That said, the amount of teaching by the mentor is ultimately determined by the mentee. You have to have goals of the relationship defined. The engagement level depends on the aggressiveness of the mentee in tackling challenges established by the mentor. Just as leadership can be situational, so can mentoring. The amount of feedback and coaching depends on how engaged and capable the mentee is. The mentee actually defines the needs. Not just in words, but in their experience, their actions (and the need for the mentor to step in), and their goals. The mentee should engage the mentor, be open and honest about their capabilities, what they want to do, and where they think their strengths and weaknesses are. These things help the mentor shape their coaching to meet those needs. The mentor needs to remember the items discussed in the coaching section and use the Socratic Method as much as possible (without abusing it to avoid actually doing anything). Remember, the focus of this exercise is on the mentee's learning, and the mentee should be able to consider the mentor as a valuable resource without becoming dependent on them for everything.

What kind of outcomes should you expect from the mentoring relationship? When you use the skills presented in this book, and take the proper steps to define the goals, boundaries, and perhaps even the length of the relationship, outcomes will become evident. These outcomes should be documented so you can follow up on them as you work through the process. For the mentee, expectations for outcomes from this exercise would include:

- More knowledge of the organization and how it functions

- Improved problem solving skills

- Improved decision making skills

- Improved skills on handling relationships

- Better understanding of their own strengths and weaknesses

- A game plan for improving on areas that need more development

For the mentor, expected outcomes would include:
- Enhanced personal knowledge of their coaching skills

- Sharpened knowledge of the business as they coach the mentee

- Improved skills on assessing needs of those they lead and coach

- Identification of potential future leaders for the organization

And if you need motivation for having a mentoring program within your organization, outcomes for the organization will include:
- More commitment and loyalty from mentees

- Increased productivity of mentees

- Renewed enthusiasm of mentors

- Development of new perspectives by all involved

- Encourages retention of your best talent

What kind of guidelines are there for the mentoring relationship? Guidelines can actually be negotiated between the mentor and the mentee. However, certain things should be made clear. Both parties must commit to devoting adequate time and attention to the process. Assuming the mentee is hungry for knowledge, they will make it a priority. The mentor must do likewise, and not think of it as simply something they are doing out of the kindness of their heart when they have time. This is serious business. You are developing the potential future of your organization. Goals must be discussed, agreed upon, and set. Listening was talked about earlier in the book. Now is a good time to practice listening skills and understand what the mentee is truly looking for. Time is at a premium, so manage your time together wisely. Set times and guidelines for when you get together. Don't let "war stories" get in the way of the business of mentoring, nor discussions of last weekend's ball game. Everyone involved should approach this process with humility. The mentor cannot act like an arrogant know it all, and the mentee can't behave as if they are part of some chosen elect for the future. Stay focused on the purpose of the mentoring process, and do all this with humility.

How long does the mentoring process last? The answer depends on the purpose of the mentoring. If you have a mentoring program and have set goals, maybe tied to a particular project, the mentoring can last the duration of the project. It could last for a set period of time, allowing for learning to take place. It could be ongoing, even to the extent of being a lifelong association supporting the development of entire careers. The short answer is, it depends. I have helped establish mentoring relationships as well as had mentors and been a mentor. More often than not, the mentoring is for a season, a purpose is served, and then mentees move on and find new mentors that can help them in their new setting, and the mentors discover new people who need mentoring. The best feeling is when you see someone you have mentored becoming a mentor themselves, and they are executing that mentor role in a way that ensures the success of the person they are mentoring.

Some key things to remember when you are mentoring someone:

- Review the skills presented in these pages and apply them with your mentee
- Make sure that the mentee has a good understanding of the concepts of continuous improvement, humility, and self-reflection
- The best learning is not sitting "at your feet" listening to you pontificate on your greatness (remember, you should be practicing humility as well), but on the job, with short cycles of learning and regular feedback
- Make sure that you are creating steadily increasing challenges for your mentee
- As they obtain success, stretch them with the next goal
- Remember the 'Learn, Do, Coach' method in mentoring them

When pairing up for a mentoring experience, it can come about in several ways. Someone may approach you and ask you to mentor them (or you may ask someone to mentor you). I'm not keen on someone offering their mentoring to others, as these people are usually the ones that are more anxious to demonstrate how smart they are to others, rather than actually helping someone develop themselves. Whether done through a formal program or an informal request, when pairing up a mentor and mentee, it is best if they do not have a boss/employee relationship. What would be even better is if they work in different functions of the organization. This "cross pollination" in the organization will help open the eyes of both mentee and mentor on the challenges different groups deal with. It will help challenge the thinking of both members of the mentoring process, and enhance the overall collaboration of the organization due to the learning that takes place in this process.

CONCLUSION

"Now this is not the end. It is not even the beginning of the end. But it is, perhaps, the end of the beginning."
- Winston Churchill

The 7 Essential Skills have now been laid out and explained to you. Specifically, explained in the context of seeking to establish an environment of Operational Excellence within your organization. If you have read this far, I can only assume you are serious about wanting to implement Operational Excellence in your organization, otherwise you would have stopped reading at about *Skill 2: Handling Change*. So what's next?

I mentioned in the *Introduction* how this book came to be. Discovering the need to develop leadership skills in an organization comes first; only after we had started in the beginning with training the rank and file employees did we realize we were following a path that was backwards to how you should actually establish Operational Excellence. We had started by conducting projects, then educating those we worked with, then targeting the leadership. You should begin with your management/leadership first, get them onboard, educated, and supportive of the 7 Essential Skills, and then educate your people on continuous improvement methodologies. Let them start using those tools to improve how they conduct business, and have the leadership actively endorse and sponsor their actions. Knowing this, where do you go from here? How do you get started?

Start with *Skill 1: Establishing the Goal*. Define what it is you want to do, and then create a vision around it and start sharing it with your people. Don't just talk to them, but start practicing your listening skills. Accept the feedback from them, positive and negative. Thank them for that feedback. Incorporate the positive, and find a way to address the negative and turn it around. Things won't happen magically overnight, or over the next month. A serious commitment by leadership to change the culture of a single facility will take two to five years based on the level of commitment and energy expended. For an organization larger than a single facility, it could take longer, but it depends again on the commitment level and the number of people selected to be dedicated to Operational Excellence roles to help move the organization forward.

Remember that while the vision is set in stone, the goals may have to change as technology changes, the market changes, and customer needs change. Continuous change is really the new norm, and as you drive towards Operational Excellence, it should be an expected part of your organizational behavior that people embrace change. It truly is a never ending journey towards excellence. You can achieve it, but maintaining it will be the bigger challenge. This, more than ever, is where leadership counts. In pursuing Operational Excellence, sustainment is vital, or all your efforts will be for naught. I've seen and read countless stories of organizations that actually achieved the changes they desired, only to watch their organizations slowly slide back into the dysfunctional creatures they were before, all because they did not work at sustaining what they had achieved.

Once again, this is on leadership's shoulders. Continuously driving, striving for excellence, continuously developing your people, helping them constantly improve on how they do things, and listening to the voice of the customer, are all part of sustainment. If you change the culture you can change the people, and that can bring about sustainment of your improvements.

"If a company wants to change the culture, it must also develop true lean leaders who can reinforce and lead that cultural change. The best way a company can develop this is through action to improve the company's core value streams, supported by committed leaders who reinforce culture change."[7]

— *Jeffrey Liker, The Toyota Way*

It is important you remember that while you are the boss, you need to act like a leader. If you aren't clear yet on the difference, here are some examples:

> A boss drives his employees, where a leader coaches and empowers them. A boss controls his people with intimidation and fear, where a leader will encourage his people to take the initiative. A boss is about themselves and their own needs, where a leader is about the needs of the team. A boss will often use people, where a leader will develop people. A boss likes to take credit, but a leader will give credit to those who deserve it. A boss will direct his employees, where a leader will engage and work with his employees.

It is imperative that when you start this journey, you not only share your vision, but back it up with action that supports it in a positive way. There are plenty of senior "leaders" who step up and say they support continuous improvement, or Operational Excellence, and want it, but very few who go beyond the lip service and actually take actions to demonstrate their support and alter how they conduct themselves so as to truly support it. Remember this: A vision without action is only a dream. Don't just dream, do! You might be either excited about the possibilities or afraid of failure and potential backlash by your peers and those over you. I can only say that those who dare to try are the ones that are looked upon as leaders. Life is an adventure, and you can make your work life a great adventure by pursuing Operational Excellence and applying the 7 Essential Skills. I'll close by quoting part of Theodore Roosevelts' "Citizenship In A Republic" speech (April 23, 1910). Take these words to heart and dare to do great things:

> "It is not the critic who counts; not the man who points out how the strong man stumbles, or where the doer of deeds could have done them better. The credit belongs to the man who is actually in the arena, whose face is marred by dust and sweat and blood; who strives valiantly; who errs, who comes short again and again, because there is no effort without error and shortcoming; but who does actually strive to do the deeds; who knows great enthusiasms, the great devotions; who spends himself in a worthy cause; who at the best knows in the end the triumph of high achievement, and who at the worst, if he fails, at least fails while daring greatly, so that his place shall never be with those cold and timid souls who neither know victory nor defeat."

NOTES

1. Design for Operational Excellence (2012), Kevin Duggan, page 28.
2. Leading Change (2012), John Kotter
3. Toyota Kata (2010), Mike Rother, p. 155
4. The Outstanding Organization (2012), Karen Martin, pp 155-158
5. One social style test I've used on the past is from The Effectiveness Institute, Inc., in Redmond, WA. Another I learned from was given to an organization I was a part of by Wilson Learning in Minneapolis, MN. The terms I use for the four social styles in this book come from the Self-Perception Guide created by the Tracom Group in Highlands Ranch, CO.
6. Continuous Permanent Improvement (2014), Arun Hariharan, pp 97-107
7. The Toyota Way (2004), Jeffrey Liker, p. 302

Other References
SME Lean Certification Mentoring Guide (2012)

SOURCES FOR SELF-DEVELOPMENT

Below is a list of some of the books that I found very useful in my personal development of leadership skills. While these books were not the sole sources for my compiling of the 7 Essential Skills, they were key inspirational sources, and should be a part of anyone's library that is looking to improve their leadership skills. I highly recommend these books to you, the reader, as you pursue your continued self-development as a leader. I know there are many more sources out there, but I think these seven books are excellent starters.

Toyota Kata, by Mike Rother
Lead with Respect, by Michael Balle' and Freddy Balle'
The Toyota Way to Lean Leadership, by Jeffrey K. Liker and Gary L. Convis
The Oz Principle, by Roger Conners, Tom Smith, and Craig Hickman
The 4 Disciplines of Execution, by Chris McChesney, Sean Covey, and Jim Huling
Leading Change, by John Kotter
It's About Time, by Rajan Suri

ABOUT JEFF ADAMS

After years of experiencing various types of leadership styles, through sports, the military, and private industry, Jeff Adams has developed into an experienced leader in driving change and continuous improvement in a variety of roles, including as a production supervisor, production planner, change manager, contract manager, manager of process excellence, and director of quality. With a diverse background, including being a former officer in the U.S.A.F., a manager in the food production industry and in Oil & Gas, Jeff brings a wide range of experiences to the table that provides him a unique perspective for tackling issues that hold organizations back from performing at their highest levels.

Jeff has helped develop courses for Lean certification, as well as leadership courses to help managers better support continuous improvement efforts in their work areas. He is a proven leader in coaching and mentoring people to excel in their current positions, and in developing them for future advancement in their careers. Jeff holds a Bachelor's in Engineering Technology from the University of Memphis, a Master's in Human Resources Management from Troy University at Montgomery, and is a graduate of NOV University's Manufacturing Leadership Program at Rice University. Jeff is a recognized expert in continuous improvement, holding certifications in multiple continuous improvement methodologies. Certifications include: Lean Silver Certification (SME), Certified Six Sigma Green Belt (ASQ), and Certified Quick Response Manufacturing, Level I (Tempus Institute).

www.ingramcontent.com/pod-product-compliance
Lightning Source LLC
Chambersburg PA
CBHW071609200326

41519CB00021BB/6935